SIDE HUSTLE TO SUCCESS

15 WAYS TO MAKE MONEY ONLINE WITHOUT LEAVING YOUR DAY JOB

By

ROBER J. MILLER

Table of Contents

Legal Notes

Introduction

Chapter 1

  Blogging

Chapter 2

  Sharing Advice

Chapter 3

  Dropshipping

Chapter 4

  CPA Network

Chapter 5

  Profit From Ebay (Selling Hot Info Guides)

Chapter 6

  Amazon Kindle Ebooks

Chapter 7

  Affiliate Marketing

Chapter 8

  Web Hosting Affiliate Commission

Chapter 9

  Advertising On Website

Chapter 10

  Niche Blogs

Chapter 11

  Freelancing on Upwork

Chapter 12

  Selling On Ebay/Amazon

Chapter 13

Make a Course on Udemy

Chapter 14

Adsense

Chapter 15

Monetize Youtube Videos

Conclusion

Can I Ask A Favour?

Bonus Chapter

How To Market Your Kindle Ebooks

About The Author

LEGAL NOTES

*Dedicated to every person who wants to leave the clutches of the corporate world and live a life of an entrepreneur. This means making real differences in the world, making money work for you instead of the other way around. I hope you guys enjoy this book and please **don't forget to rate and review.***

INTRODUCTION

You will be amazed at the amount of people making a full time living online in the US. There are people (ordinary just like you and me) making more in a month than some people do in a whole year. In this book I will show you tactics and strategies that people use to see this success.

The key here is passive income. This means you input little to no effort and make money in doing so. Imagine lying down in a beach resort somewhere with your family, sipping on some nice champaign and just enjoying the moment. You'd think "Oh how wonderful that would be, but isn't it a bit out of my budget?"

Ask yourselves what if you could do that all the while generating income at the same time. This is the exact idea of earning passive income. You don't work for the money. The money works for you

This book is dedicated to every person who wants to leave the clutches of the corporate/working world and live a life of an entrepreneur. This means making real differences in the world, making money work for you instead of the other way around.

I'm pretty sure most of you have had the thought come across you at least once in your life about leaving your day job. Let me show you how you can do that.

Chapter 1

BLOGGING

Blogging is an art you can master without any technical or computer skills. So, if you want to make money blogging, here are the basic steps to follow. It is not hard but it is doable!

Set Up Your Blog

If you want to make money blogging, obviously you will need a blog. If you don't already have one, simply follow these steps I have outlined below.

a. Buy a host

A host provides server space for your site so people can find you on the internet. Since, you are starting as a beginner with little or no experience, making use of WordPress.com or Blogger is better although they do not allow you to earn common forms of blogging income. When you become more experienced, then you can opt for self-hosted WordPress site.

On the other hand, if you have the money to buy a domain, which will be the best because you will undoubtedly, get the best value for your money. So, it would be ideal if you go for self-hosting. A friendlier website hosting company such as Bluehost is the best for you.

b. Choose your hosting plan

Choose the hosting plan you would like to start with. The Performance plan is good because you get more features that will last for a while. Since you are starting the blogging job as a new person, I recommend you opt for the Starter package. You have the option of upgrading at any time.

c. Choose a domain

A domain is a web address that can be used to find your website. So, you should register for domains of .com extension because they are more viable and result-oriented for business.

d. Choose a hosting plan

Choosing a hosting plan is based on how far you want to pay in advance. With Bluehost you can either pay for one year or a reasonable monthly amount which is not bad for your own blog or website.

e. Install WordPress

With the login details provided to you by Bluehost, log into you cpanel and click the install WordPress icon under website builders. After installation, ensure you take note of your WordPress login credentials.

Write quality content

Once you have your blog running, use your expertise and experience to write informative posts and articles that associated to your chosen topic. Make sure your content is made up of excellent quality. To be able to some make cash, you will need visitors, and the best bait to get potential visitors is that your content must be informative to your visitors. Writing of articles for your blog is the time consuming part. It will be a while before you start seeing an income.

Reach out to people in your niche

Start building genuine and sincere relationships with your readers as you engage in content writing by posting them via social media sites, making comments on other peoples' blogs, as well as forums. You can communicate with the people in your niche. Find people who could use the information you provide and get to know them as well as interact with them while building friendly relationships with them. You can offer helpful tips of your expertise.

 Reaching out to the people in your niche is so important because of the following reasons:

• People will naturally find you without you putting in yourself on the line to draw them to your site.

• You will become reputable, trustworthy and people will always be on the lookout for you information as regards their own problem.

• It's very possible those people you communicate with will likely become enduring friends and support you in the future without you requesting for it.

Increase your content

Keep growing in the knowledge of your expertise so the content you produce gets increasingly great and enriching. Use your blog to get exposure, build authority, gain trust and be helpful. Only think about making money once you have earned trust. A lot of people want to rush to the money part, but if you try to hurry yourself into monetizing before you have really built your platform, you run the risk of damaging the good reputation you so desperately need.

Monetize your blog

This is the part you may have been waiting for and it is the actual ways people make money by blogging. So many avenues of creating wealth bloggers are abound for bloggers. Each blogger has a different combination of income streams. There are endless opportunities and possibilities of making money. Your job is to find a combination that works for you.

The following is a list of income streams available to bloggers and it is divided into five major categories:

• Advertising which involves display of ads, Google Ad sense, reviews and giveaways, etc.

• Affiliate marketing which involves the promotion of another person's product.

• Digital products, this entails the sale of audio/video, apps, plugins, domains, ebooks, etc.

• Physical products which involve the selling of manufactured products, homemade products, etc.

• Services such as virtual assistant, consultant, adviser, app developer, etc.

CHAPTER 2

SHARING ADVICE

Everyone has their unique way of doing things and usually has many pieces of advice to give. Maybe you like to simplify your life by making things simple for yourself as well as others. Why not make money sharing your tips and ideas on things you love to do. Read on to find out how to make some cash while you passionately give somebody a tip.

Getting paid for the advice you give works in a simple and easy way. So many question and answers style websites exist on net where people seek answers and advice just about any situation you can think of.

In order for you to get paid while giving advice online, you have to sign up with some of these sites for free. Then, whenever there are people looking for a piece of advice as well as help about any concept you are very conversant with, you simply provide them with your knowledge and skill that are relevant and peculiar to their situation. That is how you get paid to post advice and answers.

This is an ultimate way of making money online. While surfing on the internet I had found various websites on which to get paid for answering questions. So, if you are ready to get paid for advice, I present to you a few sites where you can make money by giving advice:

Smallbizadvice

This site is for business gurus. So, if you are an expert in any kind of business or subject, it will be a good idea to earn money by sharing your knowledge in your leisure time. SmallbizAdvice can pay you for proffering advice. You can cash-out on this site after every 2 weeks. They will pay you via paypal.

ExpertSeoForum

This site is really fantastic in the sense that you will get paid for answering any SEO question. This is beneficial to bloggers, the reason being that they know much more about SEO (search engine optimization). So, if you have knowledge about search engine optimization then this site is the right place for you to make money online.

Daytipper

You must submit your work as they direct and every time you submit a tip, you are selling it to daytipper and if your tip or idea is accepted, you are selling all future rights to your tip. You will be paid a tangible sum of money.

Justanswer

Justanswer will give you customized answers from experts according to your price. The price for each questions ranges anywhere from $5 up to $25 or more. If your answer is accepted, the money is deposited into your account and you can cash out through PayPal once you reach a minimum $20. This site has an average membership of 9 million people and every nine second, one question is answered.

Ammas

You can get rewards to ask good questions and make handful of online income for giving correct answers and advice on Amma. Ammas has existed for more than 20 years. So you can trust it.

CHAPTER 3

DROPSHIPPING

Have you ever wondered how big sellers on the internet offer brand new items through dozens of posted auctions at the same time? Alternatively, most big Amazon sellers always feature more than 100 items on their websites, have you ever wondered why? Perhaps, you have been thinking about how and where these marketers get their products and are able to sell them at very affordable price. How much do you think that they make in such business deals? Nevertheless, these top sellers get their bulk products through a business retailing strategy called drop shipping.

What Is Drop Shipping?

Drop shipping is a special type of retailing technique that empowers the retailer to keep no product or item in stock but rather transfers the role for keeping product and fulfilling customer orders to a wholesaler or distributor. The retailer typically makes his or her money from the difference in retail and wholesale price of the product. On the other hand, the wholesaler or distributor makes money by having a seller that can sell product quickly.

So, anyone can get started with drop shipping and make money from it no matter your status in the society. There are no government rules against drop shippers when once you are doing it in a legal way and you do not need a special license to start listing wholesale items on your website or an auction site such as eBay.

Pros of Drop Shipping

There are two important advantages of drop shipping and they are as follow:

• You do not need get a place to hold inventory or even fill your house with products that may get stolen or damaged in the process.

• You do not have to ship anything, your wholesaler or distributer shoulders the responsibility to ship sold-out products or items saving you time and cost of going to post office as well as problems associated with weighing of products.

Cons of Drop Shipping

You have little control over the product that has been shipped out. So, you are going to have difficult describing to the customers the nature and kind of what you have ship especially if you are required to give more information concerning that particular product.

You have little control over the shipment. Supposing the product so shipped gets loss or damaged along the way or in transit, it is your duty to work with your wholesaler or distributor to rectify the issue or face negative review.

Steps To Take To Start Drop Shipping

1. Make your research to find products

Make a research to find a section or category you want to sell in and make notes of how much each item goes for. For example, if any product you want to sell is selling on $15 as an average price; you can compare prices from sites such as bestbuy and borders to know how much they would be there.

2. Test samples

Once you have chosen a product, and then go to Alibaba to buy it. Search many companies, test samples, get a good and competitive price; in fact get the best product you can find.

Tip: Selling quite an excellent product will make you lots of money.

3. List your products

You are free to list any amount of product with no upfront fees on Amazon. So, getting a professional account for the price of $40 a month so you can lower your selling fees is not a bad idea. Just sign up with Amazon advertising which will get you a free $100 Adwords voucher for promoting your product for free.

Tip: Look for better, cheap and effective ways to promote your product. You can discontinue any method that is less effective and continue with the more effective one.

4. Maintain competitive pricing

You don't have to be the lowest price in order to make your first sale and subsequently, rather consider products based on their relevance and value to customers, you can even sell tons of products that are on the third and fourth pages.

5. Provide excellent customer service

It is your duty to offer the best customer service to your prospective customers and then go extra miles further to meet their needs, but do not go overboard. Make use of quickest shipping available to start your drop shipping business and add hand written notes as well.

Tip: Ask for customer reviews for any product sold.

6. Know your stock level

As a matter of importance, you should know the levels of your stock. This is very obvious because if you lose sight of this fact, you will be out of stock when sales increase. And when that happens, you will make no money.

7. Dropship from any retailer.

So once you get the cost from the retailer but just ensure you will be profitable after fees. You can use an Amazon calculator to research about your costs, Google it.

8. Request payment daily.

If you are on tight budget to cover the cost of your orders, you can request a cash request straight to your bank account daily from Amazon. After you get this money lodged into your bank account, then go online and make order for your customers' product from the lowest priced retailer.

9. Switch to FBA

It is cheaper for you to use FBA or you get more sales through Prime. So, switch to FBA only if it makes sense to do so for your product otherwise you are just busy making more money for Amazon.

Tip: Remember to request that the price not be seen when you ship it especially when you order from your online retail store.

CHAPTER 4

CPA NETWORK

CPA stands for Click-Per-Action (CPA) and they are those networks that provide some of the quickest and simplest ways for affiliate marketers to make big money online.

Big time advertisers such as Netflix, eHarmony, Liberty Mutual Insurance or any other company are always on the lookout for new leads and are willing to pay for those services. How much you earn is dependent on the company and the offer. Generally the price per lead is about $10 to $20. CPA Networks serve as the agency between advertisers and affiliate marketers who can provide these leads.

In a nutshell, CPA marketing is when you make people take some action such as submit an email, and you get paid for that action taken. It is the easiest way to make some quick and cool cash online with little to no money to invest. You don't have to be an expert to do it, neither do you have to run a site, although if you already have a site you will do better when it comes to CPA networks' approval.

So you want to make money online? Let's see how to make money using a CPA networks.

Now, this is a height that can be cumbersome to attain, particularly if you do not have a website. But that does not mean that it is impossible to get approved for a CPA affiliate account.

Apply To a CPA Network

The best and most friendly CPA networks to apply for are Peerfly and MaxBounty as well as other friendly ones. The above mentioned sites are relatively easy to get approved and are presently ranked as one of the top CPA networks. In order to be approved for an affiliate account, there are a few things that you will have to include in your information.

Tip: Always Be Honest!

While it is important for you to be as honest as you can be with these affiliate networks, it is quite essential that you are able to lie a little bit in your application. How do I mean by this?

Well, I mean that you are going to have to do some cover up of your application slightly to make it look like you are an experienced marketer even when you are not. You will have to show the approval staffs going over your application that you have all it takes to succeed and to promote their offers in a legitimate fashion.

Choose the right offer to promote

You must have been approved before you head to selecting the right CPA offer to promote. Nevertheless, I lack the information to tell you which offer is right for you to promote. The kind of the offer you choose will ultimately depend on the kind of traffic that you drive to it.

So, I highly suggest you promote email or zip submits because they are the easiest offers that convert most frequently. You should be aware that the quality of the traffic that you drive to these offers will result in how often and how well these offers convert.

Channel traffic to your offers

The fastest and the cheapest yet the easiest way to get traffic to your offers and get things rolling is through PPC (Pay-Per-Click). You can use the cheaper method of article writing to drive traffic to your offers. This is important, because without great exposure, you offer is bound will receive no exposure and as such you will make no money.

Keep focused and be persistent

Negative campaigns? Sure, you will have one! But do not be discouraged after a few negative campaigns. You will probably have to waste a few dollars until you get used to the system.

Reinvest you proceeds

Immediately you start making money from promoting your CPA offers, then reinvest the profit in a new perfect traffic strategy and leverage PPC until you start making enormous amount of cash. So, do not rush into wasting your profit on frivolities rather buy traffic and send it to those offers, since you would already know what works.

Lastly, making money with CPA offers requires dedication; it is not a business for time-wasters or procrastinators. Just sitting one place and nursing the thoughts of what you can do, will not earn you a dime. So, the ideal thing to do right now is to take action and dive in!

CHAPTER 5

PROFIT FROM EBAY (SELLING HOT INFO GUIDES)

Selling information products can be a great way to make additional money from your readers online. It requires you to have a niche where people are hungry for information among other things, and you can put together something that attends to their needs, you are actually assured to do well by creating an ebook or some other information product for your followers. The money starts to flow when you make sales.

As a novice who is eager to make money online, how do you go about putting together an information product as well as make money in the process? Here are a few steps on how to go about it.

Consider what your customers want

Another great way to come up with an information product that is going to last for long would be to just know from your readers what they really need to know about your niche! You might be surprised by their answers, and they may come up with something that you never thought of before!

Research about the topic

Alternatively, you can create an information product that is going to be a big hit by simply asking your readers what they really want to know concerning your niche! You might be surprised by their answers, and they may come up with something that you never thought of before!

You can go about this in a few different ways. First, you can just throw a question in a blog post and allow people to make their own comments on what they would like to know more about in your niche or what their biggest queries could be.

Another option is, if you have been nursing a few ideas in your mind and you are just trying to pick the best one, you could conduct a poll on your website to let your readers vote on which one they view as the best product. Also, you could throw a question across to your readers via social media about what type of products they would be most likely to buy or read.

Figure out the right topic

Now, the first thing you will need when putting together a hot-selling info guide is a topic which people are interested in and would want to read and get more information on. A great way to know what this might be is to think about what it was that you needed to know when you started out in your niche.

Save it in a particular format

When people think of information products, they usually hold a notion of an ebook in pdf format. But suffice it to say, there are plenty of other media you can use to package your information product nowadays.

Many presenters will now use video to display their info guides. The information product can be packaged in form of a video that was recorded, or it could be presented in a slide show done in real time while the presenter speaks into the microphone. Some people may even forgo audio or a podcast and showcase the information in that format for listeners.

Of course, there is nothing wrong with an ebook format and majority of online marketers if not most folks still make use of it. On the other hand, you could attach an audio or a video presentation to it as well.

Showcase the info product for sale

Finally, get it out there in front of your loyalists, and stop wasting time trying to perfect everything! It does not have to be perfect. It just needs to be a good, informative product

Once the product is done, you need to decide how to sell it exactly. You can offer your information products for sale in eBay as well as in Amazon marketplace. There are high profit margins in these market places if you maximize the opportunity.

If you will follow the above steps, you can bet that you will produce a killer info guide that you can stand the test of time in a short while and most importantly make you enough money.

The eBook industry has grown absolutely large and is still growing exponentially each year. We are projecting that there will be significant increase in the sale of eBooks in the first quarter of this year as compared to that of the same quarter last year. So, now is best time to start writing or distributing your eBooks right for income!

CHAPTER 6

AMAZON KINDLE EBOOKS

The process of making money on Kindle is quite easy. What you do it to sign up for a free KDP (Kindle Direct Publishing) account. With your KDP account, you can simply add a new book to your bookshelf without waste of time.

You easily fill in the book title, name of the author, description of the book, upload a cover, upload your e-book file, select the price of your book and click publish. KDP will review your book within a day and will publish it by making it available for sale on Amazon around the world.

Amazon does most of the selling and marketing for you, while paying you a royalty of up to 70% for every sale. That's all about making money selling Amazon kindle books online in a nutshell.

What Is The Worth Of Each Sale?

KDP has two royalty options: 35% and 70%. If you are pricing your book anywhere from $2.99 to $9.99, then, it qualifies for 70% royalties. On the other hand, any cost ranging from $0.99 to $200 falls into the 35% royalty category.

So, since Amazon does the selling and marketing for you, you don't have to fold your hands and do nothing. You have to put in your work by coming up with a book idea or topic, getting your book cover ready, write the content or pay somebody else to write for you and plan on how to market you book. Take the following steps to kick-start your KDP business:

Choose a profitable niche

The secret to finding a profitable niche is finding one that has a large market share with low competition. One of the biggest things that I have found that determines the success of one Kindle book over the other is the niche or market that book is in. There are some book ideas that you might come up with that the market is not big enough for them.

In the same vein, you might come up with a book idea that has the potential for a big market, yet the competition is too fierce so it would be hard to get your book noticed.

Conduct market research

The first step to take is to see if there is actually a market on Amazon that will favor your book idea. This is a big mistake a lot of marketers and publishers make, as they usually create a Kindle book without doing the proper market research. I have made mistakes in the past of following the awkward step, by publishing a Kindle book without doing proper research, to later find out there is no market for the book and it generates nothing in sales. As a result, this is another important step, so it is not to be over-looked.

One of the ways to do this is by typing the keyword for the book idea in the search bar on Amazon.com and select Kindle Store when doing the research, so that your search results will display only Kindle products and not products from the entire Amazon.com

Create a captivating title and attractive ecover

Once you have decided upon a niche for your Kindle book, then enter the next stage which is to creating a title and cover for your book. When it comes to creating a title, you want to make sure that your niche your keyword in it. This will help to get your Kindle book noticed and ranked in Amazon for that keyword.

You want to make sure that your title is compelling, descriptive, has benefits in it, and really is captivating. The more relevant keywords you employ in the title, the better, as your book will show up in the search results regularly. Also, you can check the competing books and try to do something different as well, so your book will stand out from the crowd.

You want to create the cover once you have arrived at the title. You could either create the cover by yourself if you Photoshop skill or you are good with graphics, but I would recommend hiring someone else to do it. There are cheap options of getting a cover made, or more expensive options. Fiverr.com is the cheapest option.

So, when you are searching for "kindle cover" at Fiverr.com, you will see so many freelancers that are ready to create a Kindle book cover for you at the cost of $5 only. Always ensure you choose someone that has good rating and has a outstanding portfolio.

Write the kindle e-book

The next step is to write your Kindle e-book, or to hire someone to do it for you. If you are a good writer and you enjoy writing, then I would encourage you to write your own book. It is not as difficult as you think. Most of the Kindle books that I sell for $2.99 are anywhere from 20-40 pages. A Kindle book of about 40 pages is not hard to write and could easily be done within a week.

If you don't like to write or don't know how, then that is not a problem about that. So many freelance writers that you can hire; that will write your book for you at a cheaper rate and do all of the research to put it together, are always available for hire. You can look get the services of a freelance writer from upwork, elance or iwriter and other freelance writing platforms for a price ranging from $25 to $50.

Once you have your book written, you need to put it into the Kindle format before publishing.

Publish the kindle e-book on Amazon

Once the cover and Kindle book ready, you are ready to publish it on Amazon. All you need do is sign-up for a KDP account and click on the bookshelf. Click on add new title and follow the instructions.

CHAPTER 7

AFFILIATE MARKETING

What is Affiliate Marketing?

Let's get started with understanding the meaning of affiliate marketing. Affiliate marketing is a way for you (the affiliate) earn a commission for recommending products or services to your friends or readers.

To simplify it, here is the **four step process** for how it works:

1. You find a product you want to promote

2. You sign up with the affiliate company

3. You get a link which allows the merchant to track the people who clicked your link

4. You get a commission when they buy the product.

Affiliate marketing can get a bit confusing, but in this post we are just going to begin with the basics and get to where you are ready to make your first commission.

How Does Affiliate Marketing Work?

There are so many ways to track affiliates these days, but all are based on someone clicking your special tracking link and the most common type of tracking is through a cookie.

When the link is clicked, a small file called a cookie is saved on their machine which lets the merchant know that if a sale is made, it came from you.

Physical Products

The easiest products to promote are physical products and probably for one reason, and that reason is:

Amazon has an affiliate program that seems to be the largest in the world, and you are can get a link for selling any product on the site, once you sign up and earn a commission on it!

Commissions on physical products are significantly low, owing to the factors that influence selling them such as manufacturing, wholesaling, shipping, and others.

So you can earn a commission of 4% on any product at Amazon. Once you have referred at least 7 items in a calendar month, your earning will increase to 6% or 7% up to a maximum of around 8.5%.

Even if you are selling thousands of items monthly, you are still making less than a 10% commission. Because of this, a lot of people make a little bit of money off Amazon, but few who make thousands.

You can imagine, average physical product commissions are in the range of 4-10%. Anything over 10% is very good. So, if you want to promote physical products, there is probably a better place to do it than Amazon.

Information Products

An information product is the next type of product you can promote.

This information product is usually created by a blogger as well as a marketer. There are a lot of reasons why information products have proven effective to promote in Amazon:

• They are often highly priced, which means higher earnings

• They have a personality which builds trust and makes them easier to sell

• They can have complete marketing strategies that helps in sales

• Also, they solve a problem.

Realistically, becoming an affiliate can be a bit hard for these products because often the creator introduces protective measures against who they allow to market their products.

There is also no central place you can go to join, like you could with Amazon. Usually you will need to talk to the product creator directly. Alternatively, you can find an "affiliates" page on their product site.

So if you have a course or product that you have personally used and seen a lot of success in, check and see if there is an affiliate program because if you are going to recommend it anyway, you might as well get paid when people buy it!

Services

This is another big one for me, because of the kind of thing I write about here.

My business does not function without hosting, a theme, email software and the likes. So it can be easy to make a sale on services, because if I personally love and use them, there is that likelihood you will use them too.

One thing that makes services unique for instance is that often there are recurring commissions.

Promotion Techniques

By now you should have a good sense of what affiliate means, know the kind of products you want to promote, and know how to get your affiliate links for them.

In this section we are going to look at some of the easiest and most successful ways to promote an affiliate offer.

Create The Resource Page

To bring in a few sales in a few days' time, you need to create a resource page. There are tools, products, and services that you use for your blog or business. So, by creating a page of all of your tools and resources, you are creating something that is sharable, as well as useful.

A Few More Tips

If you abide by these strategies above, you will be making huge sales in your affiliate business without delay. To improve your chances even more, I have got a couple more useful tips.

Make Use Of A Beautiful Link

Generally affiliate links are pretty ugly. They are long links that often go to a secondary domain, and are pretty clear that they are affiliate. Download a plugin that will make your links look much friendlier.

Maintain Good Relationship with Your Affiliate Manager

Majority of affiliate programs for physical products or services usually have an affiliate manager that helps you generate more sales.

You will need to prove to them that you are capable to deliver, but try to contact them through phone before you begin promoting anything. They will be able to give you a good sense of what works, and potentially even give you a boost in commissions.

CHAPTER 8

WEB HOSTING AFFILIATE COMMISSION

The way to making profit from a web hosting affiliate program is with powerful promotion. This article shows a four stage plan to facilitate your web hosting affiliate business, including numerous free and low-cost advertising techniques. Study the following action steps for increasing affiliate profits, from choosing the best web hosting affiliate program to attracting potential customers.

Promote spectacular hosting services

Although your aim as a web host affiliate is to get as much commission as possible as, be informed that the web hosting provider with the highest paying affiliate program is not the best to join. What should be of concern to you is the quality of the web hosting service the company will provide to customers rather than the commission paid.

So, when customers become satisfied with their web hosting, then they will announce it to their friends as well as recommending that web hosting provider or web hosting service to them. But when customers are not satisfied with the quality of service provided by their web hosting, the reverse becomes the case.

They will announce that too and post their negative feedback everywhere in forums, social media and blog posts, costing you future customers and damaging your business reputation.

What do you think makes a good web hosting provider? Well, your guess is as good as mine. You should consider a web hosting provider with quality network facility, fast and thorough technical support, data and network security, quality of guarantee of uptime, and customer satisfaction. So, look for an affiliate web hosting program that follows a reliable payment schedule in order to be successful as a web hosting affiliate.

Also look to see if your commission will ever change according to the amount you sell. This is important because some companies do reduce the commission you earn as you become more successful, which can affect your overall income.

Select an affiliate hosting promotional package

In order for prospects to sign up for web hosting through your affiliate links, then you should access where the links are pointing to for a successful sale. There are three main choices for web hosting affiliates. They are: a landing page, a promotional website, or a promotional blog.

Landing page

This is the easiest option. Landing pages are usually supplied by the web hosting provider and tend to be designed and written for one major purpose: to facilitate immediate and convenient sign up from interested viewers. With a landing page, the affiliate hosting provider should be careful of writing the page to optimize conversion rates as well as allow you to freely promote your web hosting affiliate program. You can drive a lot of traffic to your landing page just by placing links in important locations.

Promotional website or blog

Set up your blog by writing relevant article such as reviews of web hosting and contents on your site. In this case, websites do not need much content as in the case of blogs and consequently, they may get fewer views in search engines. Generate traffic to your blog by ranking well in Google and other search engines as well as placing links in strategic places.

Drive traffic to your promotional package

If you are using a landing page as your promotional platform, placing affiliate ads and links in places that your customers have great dominance is more valuable. Add a web hosting affiliate link in your signature when performing the following activities such as:

• Posting on forums

• Posting comments on blog

• Answering questions on "Question and Answer" sites such as Yahoo! Answers.

Put banners as well as ads in an article directory about web hosting. Always make use of social media sites to offer helpful information and link to your landing page when appropriate.

When using a blog as a tool for your main promotional platform, use the tips on linking described above, but link to your blog rather than a landing page. Increase your search engine ranking by filling your affiliate site with contents that are relevant to web hosting. Also, you can create more useful links from contents on a different blog.

Make use of well-designed banners and ads

The tools you have for web hosting affiliate marketing have great influence on your potential customers as they view and click on affiliate hosting adverts. Important factors such as size, style, and message are all important when you want to choose the best hosting affiliate advert. A link in an article directory will be much smaller than a banner on your website.

Always place banners in different locations such as a side panel or at the end of an article post for web host affiliate program blogs. The ads should be captivating and eye catching, but not irritating. So, consider the size and placement carefully. You can use surrounded text to encourage web visitors to click for more about the affiliate web hosting services.

CHAPTER 9

ADVERTISING ON WEBSITE

Without doubt, **Google Adsense** is the easiest way bloggers make money especially through their sites. Majority of the new blogs with a tangible amount of traffic usually set up Google adverts on their blog sites. But there are times when Google Adsense becomes less important income generation option. However, there are other alternatives to Google Adsense that you can use to make a killing on the internet. Let's take a look at these methods of advertising on website and making money thereafter.

Pay per click advertising

Pay-Per-Click (PPC) ads, also known as Cost-Per-Click or CPC, are one of the most popular means of advertising on the internet. It is a situation where an advertiser will pay you once someone clicks on their advertisement. A lot of sites offer such services but the following seem more reliable:

Media.net is another big alternative to Adsense which is controlled by the strong network of Yahoo and Bing. They display contextual ads which focus on relevant keywords and that takes some time before they become highly optimized for your website. The continued use of this network will soon make the algorithm to determine the best keywords necessary for your audience with regards to the clicks generated.

Media.net provides a dedicated account representative who can also suggest you ways to making more income from your ads. The money transfer options are wire transfer or Paypal and $100 is the minimum amount eligible for withdrawal.

Infolinks.com is another medium through which you can implement in-text advertising on your blog. This site gives publishers a 70% income share which follows a PPC (pay-per-click) model. In-text ads are double-underlined words written on a particular page that display as ads when they are clicked.

You get paid through almost all the online payment options such as eCheck, Paypal, Wire Transfer, Payoneer and Western Union as long as you reach the minimum payout of $50 for Paypal or eCheck or $100 for Wire Transfer. So, receiving your payment is dependent on the mode of payment of your choice.

Sell your own advertising on your blog

If you are already getting a decent traffic, you may want to control everything happening and sell targeted ads on your blog. So, create an "Advertise With Us" page on your blog showing the different kinds of ads available and the amount of money it costs per month. Make sure to mention your Google PageRank, Alexa rank, and other traffic information for buyers' understanding.

Alternatively, you can use of some third-party websites to sell ads on your blog especially if you want to save yourself the hassle of selling:

BuySellAds.com is a website that deals with ads marketplace online and where you can list your ads for others to buy. They do not accept low traffic blogs so if you are just starting out, you may want to wait for at least a few months before you start seeing quality traffic.

BuySellAds.com provides for her publishers a whopping 75% of the total revenue, which is quite decent. There is no minimum threshold for payouts and you can withdraw money twice every month to your Paypal.

Sell text links on your blog

If you get good organic traffic on your blog, text-link ads are wonderful options to try. This is where you connect a few texts on your site to a page in another site.

Linkworth.com is a network that is popular with text-link and where you will find options to use rotating text ads, paid reviews etc.

Minimum threshold for payouts for those using Paypal is $25 and $100 for Check, Wire Transfer and EFT.

CPM Ad Networks

So far we have been looking at a model for ads that is mostly like CPC (Cost Per Click) model. CPC is achieved when the advertiser pays you when someone clicks your advertisers' ads. Also, CPM (Cost per Thousand) is an alternative to this and it is a situation where you are paid for every 1,000 ad impressions served.

Your income can vary largely with CPC, but that is not the case with CPM. If your CPM network sets your CPM at $5 per 100,000 impressions for instance, then you will make $500 in total when that number is reached.

Pulsepoint.com is another CPM network that is popular and where you can set your own CPM prices. For you to get accepted in their network, your website must have excellent quality of unique content. They sell mostly to a US-based traffic. So, when setting the price, always set a higher price than you profit from your backup. If they cannot beat that price, your backup is displayed. You can cash out your earnings after 45 days through EFT, Paypal or check.

Pop-ups

Granted, many advertisers and bloggers dislike popup ads although it is still an option. These ads can be displayed as pop-ups or pop-unders.

Popads offers pop-under ads and performs better with a native English speaking traffic. You can set your own price and the pop under frequency for each visitor.

You receive your earnings through Paypal, Wire Transfer and AlertPay, and you can withdraw your earnings any time. Their referral program is implemented at 10% of your earnings.

Paid reviews

You can make some good money by publishing reviews on trusted products as well as reliable services. The good aspect of this service is you command a price per review. There are websites that ask anywhere from $150 to $500 for reviews.

CHAPTER 10

NICHE BLOGS

Creating a niche blog involves nothing more than following a simple step-by-step process and these steps are enumerated below:

Decide on which blogging platform to use

You can use Wordpress (wordpress.com) because it is highly affordable and easy to use. They offer a number of blog templates you can use to quickly set up your blog. However, if you want to host the niche blog on your site, this platform offers wizards that help you do that.

Register with the wordpress blogging platform

Most blogging services are fairly easy to sign up for and start using. All you need do is to fill a form online, verify your details and you are ready to create your blog. WordPress has an interface that is user-friendly and it allows you to select any code view of your choice. In fact, you are not required to study any skill about HTML before you can create or use a niche wordpress blog.

You can register for an account with WordPress because the platform is more convenient to use.

Use blog templates to set up and customize your blog layout

As a beginner, the next thing to do is to create your page layout and selecting one of the already designed (pre-designed) blog templates. This is the easiest way to start as you can always customize it later and then start writing.

Wordpress allows you to create and edit your page layout by using drag and drop page elements. So, with wordpress, you can include Google AdSense ads within your niche blog can and even customize your blog templates. This will afford you the opportunity to make more money with your niche blog over the long run.

Start posting your content

After you have successfully set up your blog layout and you are good to go, all that is required to tap into the power of blogging is a willingness to sit down and write.

Requirements For Niche Blogging

Finally, blogging in a particular niche does not require that writers and contributors know a lot about Web page code or HTML. If you can fill in an online form, then you can blog and post comments on other blogs. It only requires your time commitment and the desire to make money out of it.

Wash and rinse this procedure to make more niche blogs. You can even master the art within a short time!

CHAPTER 11

FREELANCING ON UPWORK

You can discover how Upwork works and changed some simple things about their approach and it will make all the difference. The steps enumerated below should be useful to you as you prepare to become a successful freelancer in Upwork:

Understand upwork goals

Upwork has simple aims which are very easy to carry out. The goal of Upwork is just to link the good clients with the top performing freelancers for the success of their projects. So, all other jobs on Upwork platform is intended to increase the trust potential clients have in the freelancer they hire knowing full well that trust is the sine qua non in Upwork.

So, the valuable factors for you to focus on with Upwork are:

1. Building your credibility

2. Being relevant in the Upwork community

You build your trust by having a portfolio that is superb, looking attractive in your photo, communicating fully and clearly in your bios, passing tests that are relevant, having a successful job history, getting 5-star ratings, good client testimonials, etc.

Uncover your niche

Now that you know the mode of operation of Upwork, it becomes certain that the first assignment you should perform is to hone your pitch in order to attract and catch your most ideal and prospective clients.

This means, you need to know:

1. What end result can I give my clients?

2. Who wants that end result the most?

3. What do they need to see to believe I can do it for them?

This takes research and a little bit of soul-searching. The first step is to discover your potential niche. So, what is your niche in this regard? Your niche is that space that is perfectly located in the internet marketplace where you can do what you do best and others will pay you handsomely to deliver such jobs to them.

You discover that niche by providing accurate answers to these questions below:

1. What do I love to do?

2. That I'm great (or willing to work to be great) at?

3. That others will pay me for?

If you are honest with those questions, you will get the perfect understanding of the value you that is required by your client and precisely what you should be doing.

So, you can precisely carry out the last part which is to create a professional brand that is appealing to your clients and messaging that is directed to your clients which will make them believe you are the right person for their job.

Create and build an attractive profile

Now, having being armed with a professional brand and lots of information on your ideal clients, building your profile is a cinch. The keys here are simple:

1. Fill out your entire profile in fine detail

2. Make your entire profile relevant to the specific niche you have loads of information on.

You would be amazed with the number of freelancers who contact me asking what is wrong with their profile and when I check it is only half filled out. Also, be relevant. Every write-up on your profile should communicate the specific niche you are targeting. Don't you think so?

Get invites to bid for jobs

A great profile will help you to be displayed in the search results when clients look for freelancers related to their project. And, you will get invites to bid on jobs as a result.

As you bid for jobs, ensure you make your clients happy by doing what they want as well as communicating with them in a brilliant and friendly manner.

Finally, create these two things and you are good to go!

Delivery schedule

You will know the exact time or the length of time required to build the project and what you will have done on what days. Write that down and keep it ready for the prospective clients that will hire you.

Then, since you know the key points in your delivery, you will know the important points with which to communicate with the client. So you can build the next item below.

Communication schedule

Write down exactly the days that are favorable for you to chat with your client about key points in the delivery. Give that to your clients AND actually communicate with them on those days.

CHAPTER 12

SELLING ON EBAY/AMAZON

Selling on eBay could be the answer you have been looking for if you are looking to bring in some extra cash or maybe start a new career. You can make a lot of money by becoming part of the eBay seller community. You can invest some time to read the following steps below and you could reap a huge benefit without you knowing it.

How to Get started

Create an account with eBay.

You will need to go online and create a free account with eBay which permits you to use the online account either as a seller or a buyer.

• When the account is created, you can log in to "My eBay" and track your auctions, see bids as well as send and receive emails.

• So, you should think about the name you choose for your eBay user ID. This is how you will be known in the eBay community. Choose something that is memorable but not weird.

Consider the fees

Consider the fees because you can operate under the standard fee arrangement or choose to become a subscriber when you sell on eBay. The two major differences in fees are the number of free listing you get per month and the extra fees you will pay.

• As someone who is new to selling on eBay, you will probably want to operate under the standard fee arrangement. When your item sells, you will be charged a fee of 10% but pay no insertion fees on up to 50 listings per month. Ebay has three subscription accounts and each one comes at a slightly different cost per month.

Create a Paypal account

PayPal gives your buyers the option to use a credit card or a checking account to pay for the items they buy from you. It also allows you to sell globally. Buyers initiate the payment transaction with PayPal, and PayPal, in turn, transfers the money to your account.

• Having a Paypal account is not compulsory in order to sell on eBay, but it can be difficult to succeed without one. So, greater majority of eBay users have a PayPal account.

• If users want to search for auctions, there is a feature that allows doing that by checking a box that displays "only show sellers who take paypal." This option is common among users who don't want to be disturbed with writing and mailing a check or using some other form of payment.

Make a right choice of what to sell

It is best to start by selling things that you already have in your house. Check all the rooms individually and look for things you no longer need or wear or perhaps have never even used.

• It is ideal to look around on eBay to see what other people are selling and at what price. Check to see how many "bids" an item has so as to measure its popularity.

• Sell what you know. Not only will you need to write a detailed description of the item in your stock, but prospective buyers may get in touch with you with questions. It can be difficult to completely explain the benefits one can derive from a product as well as give answers to general questions if you are not all that familiar with the item yourself.

• Another online tool used in ebay is "Selling Inspiration House". You can use it to go through a sample home and click on items you could sell and see the amount of money accruable to you for everything from shoes to computers.

• Determine what sells well and opt for more of that product. There are sales that can be a good way to buy things inexpensively that might sell for more on eBay such as estate sales and local garage.

Start small

You want to take things one step at a time while your ultimate goal may be to become an eBay top seller. So, beginning with just a few items to sell gives you the chance to learn the ropes and establish yourself as a reliable seller in the marketplace.

• Selling on eBay may present you with some unexpected challenges, which is common with any new enterprise and mistakes are imminent. Begin by selling just a few items so you can become familiar with the challenging duties that accompany a seller.

• You need to have lots of positive feedback in order to become a truly successful seller. When you are first starting out, you won't have any. Build your business gradually and offer excellent customer service so that you can earn positive feedback. That way, you will earn the trust of buyers, who will be keen to do business with you once they see you are an established and honest seller.

CHAPTER 13

MAKE A COURSE ON UDEMY

So many resources are available on the concept of **Udemy** and they are useful in explaining the various processes involved in the creation of an Udemy course. As you may be aware, many people require this information in a detailed manner probably as a result of little data on this topic. So, I take have taken this opportunity to create this guide and provide all the necessary information that are relevant to Udemy course creation as well as how to make passive income from it.

Plan your course

It is important you plan the way you want to run your course. This is important because, he who fails to plan plans to fail. The schedule of the number of hours you commit to creating an Udemy course is very vital. Planning involves gathering of materials needed for the course such as web camera, microphone and other relevant applications. You can as well get your PC ready by installing all the needed software for both video and voice recordings.

Select the right niche

If you do not select the right niche then there are chances that your course might not get you income the way you want it to be. So, this stage is very important one. Here is how to go about it. Create a productive idea in your mind that is highly captivating and is hot and capable of attracting immediate sign ups. So, before you start the course, ensure you check Udemy to see if someone else has actually created any courses around that topic.

 Now, if someone has created any course around your desired topic then check the contents, number of students who have subscribed to it and whether it is a free course or not. These few parameters can give you a clear picture on your niche or you shift to a new niche.

Create the relevant content

Having chosen the right niche, the next step is to write informative contents that are relevant to your niche topic. Once the course is fixed then, pen down the likely areas which you can focus your attention in your course. Draft the headings and then group them in a proper way so that everything looks perfect. Start creating the appropriate content sections that complete the topic so drafted. Use references, examples and case studies wherever possible.

Creating case studies and live examples in your course will be an added advantage to make it because it will make your course more popular and getting more students.

Publish the completed work

This is the time for you to publish the course on Udemy. So, rather than uploading the videos to Youtube and then linking to Udemy, it is ideal to upload directly to Udemy server to finish up all activities smoothly and perfectly. Making your course a paid one or the free one is entirely your choice. So if you wish to create a paid course, ensure you are reasonable with the price. Higher prices might seem good to make money but in reality, it is completely opposite side of the coin. If the course is not worth as priced then it would not become a good income source.

Promote your course

There are so many ways to promote your courses to get the required number of students and invariably the income flowing. You can promote your course on these websites: Reddit, Facebook, Twitter, Ozbargain, Groupon and Mighty Deals, Slick Deals etc.

In conclusion, demy keeps 30% of the income you earn and pays 70% from the course to you. But the fact remains that you can increase your percentage earnings. How? Udemy allows instructors to promote their own courses. So whenever you promote your course using the special affiliate link, then you are entitled to get 85% of the earned income.

CHAPTER 14

ADSENSE

Adsense is an advert that runs in designated sections of your website. So, advertises pay Google to run ads on your site and get a percentage of that pay. Alternatively, when advertisers pay Google to run their ads on Google display network through the Google Adwords program, their ads will display on the participating websites through Adsense slots.

So, how do you benefit from this income stream? It is by becoming a partner with Google through their Adsense program. What you need do is to sign on with Google as long as you have a website of your own.

Explained below are the steps to take in order to start running Adsense program and making money from it.

Understand the importance of personal website

Google has made it mandatory that you must be the owner of the website submitted for Google Adsense application and this must be proved before your application is granted. Nowadays though, Google now has a second level of verification, making things a little bit more difficult. It further translates that the publisher must prove that they own the web site that they intend to run ads on. This has made it compulsory for any person wishing to run Adsense on his or her website to get a website.

Register a domain name

The strategy here is: buy a domain name and attach it to a free website creation service, that's all. How do you actualize it? Nowadays, it is easy and simple to own a domain name as well as create a website of your own.

So, the tendency of going through the technicalities of getting your own hosting and building a web site is zero, although it can be cheap when using WordPress. In reality, you can get a domain for $10-$15 for one year from Namecheap.com as well as build a free new web site on Weebly.com. Having done this, you should attach the new domain name you bought to your newly created web site.

So, how do you generate income from the kind of ads that shows up in the ads slot?

Keep in mind that you are giving control of a certain portion of your web site to Google to do what pleases them as regards running of adverts. You have to exercise some control over parameters such as appearance, size and other. Additionally, you have the ability to block ads. Also, you can decide if the ads are text, images or animated. There may be other kinds as well.

Apply for an Adsense account

Now, to apply you will need to have your web site setup already. Setting up your website means buying your own domain name and filling it with relevant content. Then, go through the app process by using your Google account (i.e. Gmail or YouTube account).

Google will let you know if your site qualifies for approval or not after they might have peeped at it. If so, you will place the Adsense code on your site and the code will be blank firstly after placement on your site. Once an ad shows up, you know that your account has become active. So, when your account is active you can create new ads to run on other sites

The process of getting your apps in place could take a couple of days if not weeks or longer. Just be patient and wait it out. Google sends message to your email address informing you of each stage so that you will know the stage you are currently. If you don't see an email for quite awhile it may have been lost. That is possible.

You can take a quick look at your AdSense account and you will see messages across the top indicating the stage you are in.

Enjoy your new income stream, some people have made and is still making a living out of it!

CHAPTER 15

MONETIZE YOUTUBE VIDEOS

Adsense is an advert that runs in designated sections of your website. So, advertises pay Google to run ads on your site and get a percentage of that pay. Alternatively, when advertisers pay Google to run their ads on Google display network through the Google Adwords program, their ads will display on the participating websites through Adsense slots.

So, how do you benefit from this income stream? It is by becoming a partner with Google through their Adsense program. What you need do is to sign on with Google as long as you have a website of your own.

Explained below are the steps to take in order to start running Adsense program and making money from it.

Understand the importance of personal website

Google has made it mandatory that you must be the owner of the website submitted for Google Adsense application and this must be proved before your application is granted. Nowadays though, Google now has a second level of verification, making things a little bit more difficult. It further translates that the publisher must prove that they own the web site that they intend to run ads on. This has made it compulsory for any person wishing to run Adsense on his or her website to get a website.

Register a domain name

The strategy here is: buy a domain name and attach it to a free website creation service, that's all. How do you actualize it? Nowadays, it is easy and simple to own a domain name as well as create a website of your own.

So, the tendency of going through the technicalities of getting your own hosting and building a web site is zero, although it can be cheap when using WordPress. In reality, you can get a domain for $10-$15 for one year from Namecheap.com as well as build a free new web site on Weebly.com. Having done this, you should attach the new domain name you bought to your newly created web site.

So, how do you generate income from the kind of ads that shows up in the ads slot?

Keep in mind that you are giving control of a certain portion of your web site to Google to do what pleases them as regards running of adverts. You have to exercise some control over parameters such as appearance, size and other. Additionally, you have the ability to block ads. Also, you can decide if the ads are text, images or animated. There may be other kinds as well.

Apply for an Adsense account

Now, to apply you will need to have your web site setup already. Setting up your website means buying your own domain name and filling it with relevant content. Then, go through the app process by using your Google account (i.e. Gmail or YouTube account).

Google will let you know if your site qualifies for approval or not after they might have peeped at it. If so, you will place the Adsense code on your site and the code will be blank firstly after placement on your site. Once an ad shows up, you know that your account has become active. So, when your account is active you can create new ads to run on other sites

The process of getting your apps in place could take a couple of days if not weeks or longer. Just be patient and wait it out. Google sends message to your email address informing you of each stage so that you will know the stage you are currently. If you don't see an email for quite a while it may have been lost. That is possible.

You can take a quick look at your AdSense account and you will see messages across the top indicating the stage you are in.

Enjoy your new income stream, some people have made and is still making a living out of it!

CONCLUSION

Looks like you made it. You're now an expert, give yourself a pat on the back. What's the next step? Let's take a look at what Nike says about that – "Just Do It."

That's exactly what you have to do next. Don't wait around, there are tons of ways you can make money online and I just showed you the tip of the iceberg. Take one of these chapters and topics that I taught you, and start implementing right away, like LITERALLY right now.

Follow my step by step action plan in the relevant chapters and START. And as always, if you need any support or you have any questions or concerns, you can always visit my blog (earnsixfigurenow.com) and reach me there.

Can I Ask A Favour?

If you enjoyed this book, found it useful or otherwise then I'd really appreciate it if you would post a short review on Amazon. I do read all the reviews personally so that I can continually write what people are wanting.

If you'd like to leave a review then please head on over to this book's Amazon product page.

Thank you very much for your support!

BONUS CHAPTER

HOW TO MARKET YOUR KINDLE EBOOKS

The elementary principles of marketing and promotion are pretty much identical for an e-book as for a tangible book. When marketing e-books, it's ideal to do it online. There are quite a few nice strategies to assist you in this extremely important process.

Pricing makes a huge difference. Having a general understanding of what is actually selling in the market helps to make sure you're reasonably within the competitive range.

Here are the average prices of various kinds of works on Amazon:

- The average price of a hardcover book on Amazon is about $9.99
- Books that are on the market as trade soft covers often are priced from $5.99 to $7.99 as the Kindle editions
- Big market paperbacks generally cost around $2.99-$4.99
- Monthly subscriptions to magazines and newspapers are within the range of $9.99$14.99
- One magazine issue is within the $1.49-$2.99 range
- Some big name magazines are about ½ price of offline subscriptions
- Blog monthly subscriptions are about $0.99 with a typically free 14-day trial
- Articles that are by themselves and other short form works are $0.99-$2.99

How to Choose a Price

Theoretically, the lower the price on a book, the higher the conversion rate should be. Similar to selling products on websites, people have to know that your site exists as the first step; you can have the most sophisticated, creative, and high quality site out there, but if people have no idea it exists, what good is it? This concept works identically with e-books.

Here are some pricing tips for works you're selling:

- For diminutive length stories or works or articles, price it from $0.99 to $2.99
- For books, start low and change as needed
- It is highly suggested to not charge more than $9.99 for a usual novel-length book
- Softcover books should run from $2.99-$7.99
- Books only available in digital form should be priced with good judgment
- Depending on the niche your book is in, it may get by with being more expensive than the standard price; usually, these kinds of books deal with something very scientific, are saturated with a lot of graphics, or may be justified if you have to reimburse people who helped with the work.

Amazon Sales Rank

Amazon shows how great a work is performing via the sales ranking system. It's modified by the hour and is computed based on current and past sales information. In order to thin down a product's sales results, items are graded by how great they are performing in their solo niches with category sales ranks.

Standard sales rank is different because it displays how great a product is selling as a big picture. Only writers publishing via the KDP can see their sales reports in their own accounts.

How Sales Rank Works

The more people purchase your product in the Kindle store, the higher chances your work will become very recognizable in your niche. The more sales you make, the more exposure your work will get. It will be difficult to make it to the top ten, but even if you make it to the top 100 or even 500, your exposure and sales will enhance tremendously.

Customer reviews hold a high significance on book sales; poor reviews usually decrease book sales and positive reviews are the prerequisite to people telling their friends, family, and acquaintances about how great your work was, meaning a lot more sales!

Transitioning into paper books

If it happens that you decide to release a title solely for the Kindle but later put forward a Print on Demand edition of that book, the sale information and review assessments for the e-book edition diffuse into the print version that is sold in the standard Amazon book store section of the site.

To ensure the formatting of your book is pleasant in the Print on Demand version, check out CreateSpace; to find it online, just put in "createspace" in the Amazon search bar to pull it up. **CreateSpace** is a supplementary company to Amazon. When you see the page, it'll allow you to register and submit works for no charge.

When you make a Print on Demand title, CreateSpace gives a free ISBN if you don't have it at the time of registering. After you acquire this number, you may use it for your current Kindle title so that the two will be connected together on Amazon.

Promotions

There are a multitude of methods to promote your eBook. Here are some strategies to use in introducing your new work:

- It is ideal, since you're a new author and have to prove yourself to your audiences, to start with a cheap introductory price like $0.99. After your book picks up the pace in sales and become trendier, you can increase the price slowly as time goes on.
- If you have a long length book, it is worth a shot to put up a small excerpt of it as being available for sale as a teaser that will persuade readers to purchase the book in its whole form. If you have a non-fiction book, you can pull out a small section of content that is very helpful, abstract, and/or not well known.

If you wrote a fiction book or other fiction based work, take an excerpt from a very exciting part of the book where it's from an escalated action point or some other highlight. The bottom line is that whatever people read in the excerpts showcased, should really incite a strong desire to read the rest of it. Excerpts run from $0.99-$2.49 and are about the length of an article from 1-5 pages.

Serializing Your Work

If you have a work (non-fiction or fiction) that is very lengthy, it's a good idea to chop it up into sections and sell them apart from each other. As a guideline, think of novelettes from about 7,000-18,000 words; novellas from around 18,000-40,000 words; books/novels as 40,000+ words.

The most important point to remember is that in your series, every chapter should be able to stand on its own "two legs," meaning that the end of the chapter should leave a cliffhanger where it begs the reader to want to read the next chapter. The Charles Dickens' books are an example of successful serialized series.

It's up to you if you prefer to finish the work completely and then start serializing it, or if you prefer to write it as you progress. After your e-book is serialized from beginning to end, you may publish it as one volume. Taking the approach of serializing can be beneficial for the promotion of your work because it can build up curiosity and eagerness while creating a flame around the series.

All of these traits can assist in wheeling in new readers. If your work qualifies as bringing in the heat to readers, it might be able to mainly rely on people telling others about it and social marketing advertisement.

Press Release

Putting out a press release may be worth a shot to include in your marketing portfolio; it could help market your e-book mainly if you're a resident in a small to medium sized city. This may help because you would be a local resident publishing a book, which may be considered exciting and attention-grabbing.

Your home-based radio stations, newspapers, and television channels might become interested in an article or interview; this exposure would be just what you need to market your book in your town. Be very methodical in choosing the newspapers or television stations you'll target by doing research on them to see if what you will offer will have a higher chance of creating interest to that station.

For example, if you are writing a book about how weather affects people's moods and health, choosing weather stations to target would be a logical decision. Don't just pick and submit to many stations without doing your homework. It is a good idea to write a cover letter to a specific person with a press release or phone call.

How to Social Network Offline

To network efficiently means to keep an eye and ear open to latest opportunities. Try your best to make the most of what opportunity comes your way, meaning how you can advertise your work in your community and in other avenues.

It is helpful to start by looking at the topic your work is about to choose where it could fit, i.e. If your work is regarding the history of reptiles, you could see if there are any zoos, aquariums, and museums in your area to tell your book about. There could also be an animal appreciation group that might be interested in promoting your e-book.

If you're a newcomer to the sport of publishing, you might want to read industry works similar to your genre, i.e. if your niche is in healthy food, check out reading magazines such as Cooking Light and other related publications so you can be familiar with similar groupings and organizations.

You could take an extract from your work and send an article to them as well. If your article is approved and published, you can request the editor to put a note that the article is selected from your Kindle book, and tag on the title and a url to the work. Be open minded with trying various ideas and always be on the lookout for promoting opportunities.

Relatives and Friends

It can't be stressed enough how important it is to let as many people know about your book via word of mouth. You just never know how its influence can affect your work immensely. Let your family and friends know all about it via a well written email! They have contacts that they can send the email to and a snowball effect can happen.

Business Contacts and Professional Groups

It's a good idea to converse with your professional associates and co-workers when it's fitting to do so; a great idea is to throw a festival to rejoice in the introduction of your Kindle work. Invite workers to the party who have a matching interest to your work's topic. Think about visiting conferences with your work's industry alliances.

Take a couple of tangible copies of your book or a paper ad for your Kindle version to give out to people. Keep in mind that you should be very cautious about how you approach this kind of advertising while conversing with people. You should NOT be very pushy and force your work on anyone; it's considered unprofessional and this act could backfire and give you a horrible reputation—think of it like a website being designated as spam.

The key is to time when and how to act, i.e. if you trade contact information with an editor or publisher, be sure to contact them again in a suitable amount of time and write a sophisticated kind of letter that reminds them of your meeting so you can make sure they remember the correct person. Visit a few conferences if possible. Be vigilant in your networking and learning more data.

You may also get more involved by volunteering in some conferences; you can assist in planning one or put on your creative thinking caps and participate in some other form for a professional society. By doing this, you will get "brownie points" and not be ignored for your efforts, thus helping your reputation.

If you're timid, you are going to have to realize that you have to put yourself out there. Think of it like acting. Practice acting to help ease into the process. It may help you out first to start assisting with things that need it at first to ease yourself into it. Speak to people and trade business cards when the chance happens.

Professional Image

Two groups that are great for published writers to join because they supply a multitude of professional related assets are PEN and The Author Guild. The Author's Guild supports different and important issues for published authors like law-based services, rights' protection, and just reimbursement.

A part of this membership's obligation is that book authors must have a work from an American publisher that is reputable and who obtains a percentage of the work's sales with a large advance in which the writer is the copyright owner.

Unfortunately, if you only have a work on the Kindle, you don't qualify; however, if you signed a royalty contract on your Kindle work with a reputable American publisher that has offered a major advance, then you would meet the criteria. Bear in mind that this type of situation happening is very improbable. Other types of writers that may qualify are contributors, translators, coauthors, ghostwriters, and freelance writers.

PEN promotes open expression as its main foundation. According to its website, its members have published at least two books of "literary character or one book of exceptional distinction."

Here are some websites to some qualified societies that will help guide you:

- The Creative Penn: www.thecreativepenn.com
- John August Screenwriting Tips: http://johnaugust.com
- The Reading Edge Podcast: http://thereadingedge.com
- TeleRead: www.teleread.org ☐ PEN: www.pen.org
- The Authors Guild: www.authorsguild.org
- The Graphic Artists Guild: www.graphicartistsguild.org
- Publetariat: People Who Publish: www.publetariat.com

Blog Marketing

Remember that just having a mind blowing novel on Kindle does not mean you'll automatically be triumphant and become rich. After your publisher has verified your account and it's ready to go, then you'll have the ability to blog right from Author Central for free by checking out the Blog tab. You can blog using two different methods; one method is to go to the "Add an RSS feed" tab and put in the feed address, NOT the blog's address.

Or, you can click the Create a new post address and put in a fresh post straight to Amazon via the box that generates. To make an RSS feed using Blogger, visit your blog to sign in and click Customize at the top. Check that the "Layout" tab is chosen and go to the link "Add a Gadget." Next, include the "subscription links" tool to your blog.

Then, perform all the actions the directions state for initiating this process, which are easy as pie. This is the way to get a RSS subscription capacity included in your blog. To locate your RSS feed address, check out the blog subscription url, which is on your blog's home page.

Click on the url and find "posts;" then, choose how you want your feed to look in its layout from the options given. The next page will showcase your feed address in a url. Copy and paste this url in the proper box at Author Central to begin extracting your blog feeds into your Author Central account. There will be a note giving caution that it may take up to 24 hours for brand new posts to appear on your author page.

Videos

Amazon has a very cool feature that lets authors upload videos. Go to the "videos" tab to upload your work. The following formats are what is accepted to upload videos in: .wmv, .flv, .mpg, .mov, and .avi. A huge advantage to putting up a video on your author page would be for credibility and helping to subtly market your book, i.e. if you performed speaking expeditions, these will look great for your profile.

Another option would be to upload a video of yourself talking about your work without giving away too much to ruin it, the reasons for writing your work, and other things about your work that will incite excitement and suspense. There is something about seeing someone express their passion in "person" vs. on paper alone that allows the reader to absorb it as well.

Amazon permits files that are at the biggest 500 MB. You should go to the "content guidelines" url to check that your video meets the content qualifications. Making a video is not as complicated as it may sound because most new computers come with a built-in camera. Videorecording functions differ depending on the computer.

You can start by doing a search on your computer using the keywords "video" or "camera." If you don't have a camera built into your computer, then you can buy a latest webcam for as low as $8 from www.buy.com. You can also check out www.amazon.com to see if it has cheap webcams.

Cameras are diverse, so you should invest some time in reading the directions to learn how to set it up and record appropriately. Trust me; this'll save you a lot of heartache down the road if you just learn how to do it the right way from the start.

Take heed to the kinds of content Amazon does not allow to be posted:

- Obscene content or things that are offensive like nasty language or depicting other people in a bad way
- Promotions or advertisements
- Stuff that isn't yours to use
- Personal data like phone numbers, mailing addresses, and website urls
- Data on buying and shipping stuff, costs, and other things related
- Commentary to information that is accessible on your author page and within book reviews
- Promotions for good reviews and votes

- Plot spoilers (why would you want to do that anyway?!)

Happenings

After your account is ready to go, you'll be able to put facts regarding your speaking events, speeches, book tours, when you'll be in bookstores, and other happenings under the "events" tab. Amazon is a joint venture partner with a company called book tour: www.booktour.com They follow author occurrences, so all new events you put in your author central page will be distributed with Book Tour; book tour also gives your info to other sites/resources to give you further exposure.

To submit a new happening, go to the "create new event" section and input your description of the event, the location, the name of the work the event is correlated with, and the date and the time it'll begin. Make sure to be very specific and use loads of details as you can in the description section.

Definitely state if you'll be giving a speech on your book or similar topics because this will give you a wonderful chance to squeeze in advertising copy; the key is for it to be pertinent to the book and event bordering it. What you put in the description section needs to seduce readers into attending your event; events are a fabulous way to get exposure and demonstrate that you're involving yourself as a professional in the marketing of your work.

More on Blogs

Creating a name for yourself on the Internet is of vital importance. Amazon has a blog option as mentioned earlier, but it's relatively limited to the amount of exposure you can acquire than if you have a standard blog with one of the biggest free blog services on the net---WordPress and Blogger.

You can check these out by visiting:

http://wordpress.com

Or www.blogger.com

There is a big caveat to using a blog. You need to be honest with yourself and ask if you would want to keep posting to your blog at least once a week. A blog's main purpose is to give consistent updates and if you're not going to do that, there is no point in setting one up. It's simple to run a blog, so that's a good thing.

Here's an example of a fantastic blog by the author Anne Mini below. Read her biographic information as well to get an idea how some of these concepts stated in this book tie together. www.annemini.com. This blog contains an immense amount of helpful information that Anne wrote about grammar guidelines, manuscript layout help, and tons of other things dealing with editing, writing, and the ever evolving realm of publishing.

Your blog does not need to just focus only on your work; you can write about your experiences with your path to publishing for the Kindle, problems you may have ran into (more than likely, others can relate), overall experiences with e-publishing, marketing your work, and other various experiences with agents, editors, or publishers.

Other ideas for topics include writing about your specialize subject of comfort and a multitude of other experiences you have on a professional level of writing. Doing this will help you form a professional profile and reputation that will only enhance your future sales.

Website

Before thinking about investing funds into magazine advertisement, you should first invest money and time into a website instead. It's important to have one because so much information about yourself, works, etc can be put on there. It's ideal to have your website and blog all on one site, within the same domain name.

It is basically like your public identity as an author and a place that readers can easily check out for sources to things linked to your professional profile and work; it also helps that if someone wants to reach you that your contact info is on your site. You never want people to work too hard to be able to find you online because chances are that they will just give up and forget about it. Make it as easy as possible for people to find you online.

For some tips on what to put on your site, it helps to look at how others did it first to get an intuitive idea. It will be easiest just to hire a freelancer or friend to build one for you too on www.elance.com Here are some useful links that can help give you a lot of ideas.

www.kevinprufer.com/index.html

www.mdbell.com

www.stephenking.com

www.how-to-build-websites.com/lessonOne.php

Suggested Information to Include on your website

- Cover graphics
- ISBN
- Summary of work
- Publication date
- Target readership
- Teaser excerpt from the first chapter
- Info about how and where to purchase your book (Make sure this is clear and easy to follow)
- Commentary of your works
- Summaries of each work you've published
- Promotional excerpts by other people in the business
- Don't interweave information; this means to separate your author biographic data from your personal or other non-

author career data. The exception is if your job relates to being an author, i.e. if you're a librarian.
- Put in future dates and a chart of previous events like lecture or book tours (that you've attended or are scheduled to attend) that occurred.

As a final reminder, it's very important to keep the material on your site fresh and update at least once a week. If you find yourself in a position to not have anything to think of writing, post news and events in the business from around the internet, or your feedback to a work you've read lately. Just be in the habit (which will put your readers in the habit of checking out your site) of doing this and it'll be easy to continue after a while.

Aside from keeping readers keeping up with what you're doing, it's vital to having a lot of content on your site because this will increase the number of other sites that will link to your site; this linking is very helpful in helping to rank your site in the search engines. Making a positive impression with Google can never hurt, since it's the biggest search engine at the moment.

Now, you have a great starting point to begin your quest to becoming an accomplished author on Kindle. There are many resources available to help. Go for it!

About The Author

Robert is a writer, author, entrepreneur, life coach, personal trainer, speaker and an avid traveler.

Robert has been making money online since 2013 and decided to hop on to Kindle and share with the world his wealth of knowledge. Robert loves the luxury of being able to travel and yet make money doing so.

He always tells his clients, you don't need to think of travelling as an expense but rather as an investment.

Some of his hobbies include:

- Meditation, Mindfulness and The Meaning of Life
- Running, Biking, Swimming, Rock Climbing
- Helping Individuals Reach Their Full Potential
- Spending Time With His Family
- Playing Competitive Basketball
- Writing, Traveling, Blogging

If you want to learn more about Robert or how to earn income online, you can go ahead and visit his blog at earnsixfigurenow.com.